HEAD

HEAD by Christine Kanownik
Published by Trembling Pillow Press
New Orleans, LA
ISBN-13: 9781732364721
Copyright © 2019 Christine Kanownik

All Rights Reserved. No part of this book may be reproduced in any form without permission from the publisher with the exception of brief passages cited or for educational purposes. Reproduction for commercial use is prohibited except by permission of the author.

Typesetting and Design: Megan Burns
Cover Design: Matthew Revert
Cover Art: *The Severed Head of John the Baptist* by Rachel Stern & James Lyman, 2014
Copyedit: Kia Alice Groom

NEW ORLEANS

HEAD

by

Christine Kanownik

TABLE OF CONTENTS

THE SAINTS ARE DEAD

Wheat

Rake

Ox

Leadworts

Garlic

Privet

Hatchery

Hellebore

L'ANGE

MESSAGES FROM THE DEAD HEAD: The Devil's Own

Satanic Panic

The Labor of Being

Power of Women

I tried to write a ghost poem

The Tower

American Beauty

Look for America

Baby Hole

arms

I want to be a tree

rather than a diamond

I WANT MY BODY TO LAY SCREECHING VOID

/\/\/\/\/\/\/\/\/\/\/\/\/\/\/\/\

In which the protagonist eats naked unaware of certain tragedies

Phantom Brand

MIRACLE SONGS

DECOLLATION

A page of mourning

Agnes of Rome

Medusa

I am Jeanne

Fertility

The Cult of the Head

Everyone was afraid that they'd die

Some Experiments with Severed Heads

A night to dismember

It is worth acknowledging

Believe what I say

Music Minus One High Voice:

The ____ of Lucretia

EVERYTHING I DO IS A STATEMENT ABOUT HOW I'M GOING TO LIVE FOREVER

It takes dynamite to get me up

Revenge Head

The Head at the End of the Mind

The Executioner's Song

Salome Requesting the Head of John the Baptist on a Plate

An Invitation to Beheading

NOTES

ACKNOWLEDGEMENTS

*Death poems
are mere delusion —
death is death.*

-Tokō

Is a chicken dead when one leg is amputated?
No.
What about when its two legs are removed?
No.
Two legs and 2 wings?
No.
Thus, 'death' is not primarily a matter of loss of mass.
Is a chicken dead at the very moment of decapitation?
Some will say yes, other will say no because the headless body can still move around for a while, but in an uncoordinated way.
Then who is right?

-       Arnold De Loof

THE SAINTS ARE DEAD✝

Wheat

If only you were
a man/avenged

but then we'd have nothing
to do   but to weep for her

we
a cowardly herd without a soul

it is the toilet
of death   but it
leads

to immortality

July 17, 1793
Place de la Concorde, Paris, France

Rake

I put needles
in the bread
& milk
through supernatural means

the devil came to me
as a black dog

a neighbor had a dream about her

The Great Noise
came suddenly tho
it's always been there

up-with-the-nose
down-with-the-gut

the ghost of a DOG
guarded my garden

called noseless
cooking pies under the pot

it will be eternal light
it will be
eternal
light

April 29, 1676
Stockholm, Sweden

Ox

as for feathers
        everyone wears them

it would seem
extraordinary if I
did not

my blood remains

take it

but do not make me suffer long

October 16, 1793
Place de la Concorde, Paris, France

Leadworts

God thus became
in my mind

a vision of poetic beauty

Reader: mark that queenlike burgher-woman

I get no pleasure
from pricking bubbles or killing flies

rather chew off my own
fingers than   indulge
that pleasurable
loss of self-control

November 8, 1793
Paris, France

Garlic

Sun and moon
        have no light left

My body will not allow me
to mingle with the men
    my heart is far braver
than that of a man

Arise ! Arise !

Autumn wind, autumn rain, fill one's heart
with melancholy

July 15, 1907
Shaoxing, China

Privet

Somebody
after all
had to make a start

Such a fine, sunny day, too					and I have to go

I know that life

is a doorway to eternity		and yet my heart
so often gets lost in anxieties

It forgets the Great Way Home that lies before it

the sun still shines

February 22, 1943
Stadelheim Prison, Munich, Germany

Hatchery

It does not matter
how far we are
separated

no matter what
is taken from us:　　　　　Sir Resolute
a pint of the ordinary

In this way
we build an altar
in our own hearts

March 30, 1943
Vienna, Nazi Germany

Hellebore

Dear ladies and gentlemen:
a very indiscriminate murder has occurred
& I felt
the girl must become a painter

I want peace rather
than a diamond

this like a cloud
close your eyes
to bear it

[Note] peace now and way too quiet

January 30, 2015
Syria

L'ANGE

MESSAGES FROM THE DEAD HEAD:
The Devil's Own

One day
we're accosted by an Intruder
when we enter our home

Ah, but there's where he's wrong

We return home one day; we're accosted by intruders

*An American Story
of a young woman and her head*

As a favor to a friend
He stays with Tom, a policeman, and his wife
in New York City

*When I was separated from my head
When I returned home
to find my dead head missing*

When we come home one night
we realize that Tom is compelled
to stop him

*when I came home
and I was all dead head*

which draws an American family into crossfire
the heart of Troubles
in the basement of an honest cop

*my head cries out in panic
but I don't answer*

Trusted as a friend
They thought they brought home

The Angel

but they brought danger home instead

Satanic Panic:

I was exactly what I wanted to be—hunted

When you are driving at night, do you tend to
look in your rearview mirror more or less ?

What do you see each time ?
1. nothing
2. the Empty road
3. a dark figure in the backseat
4. headlights, approaching
5. taillights, departing
6. something you need

Tally your score

Now convert your children to the Church of Satan

I gave my body to Satan once
He never called—
but I am filled with a dark magik

The Labor of Being

The ball atop my spine keeps
        spinning
           I cannot relax or see

I dreamt that
Van Gogh plowed the fields
and painted the plowing
of the fields
in every image
of a plowed field

but still

his paintings were never
plowed fields;
no actual plower Actually
existed

I'll take his eyes with me when I pass
    We get through this by getting through this

Every stroke belies Fertility
        I am a pomegranate split open
        I am the pomegranate seeds
        I am juice spilt

I want the truth in my mouth
hard and round like a candy you cannot chew or swallow

INSTEAD:
I'm a partridge dressed for the Holiday

INSTEAD:
I am the expressive use of paint
ridiculed by my peers

INSTEAD:
my stars became a maelstrom of light

INSTEAD:
I am a dream that means Absolutely Nothing

Power of Women:

A style of art and literature emerged in the medieval and Renaissance eras. It depicted women besting powerful and clever men, sexually or physically or both. Common images were men being dominated by their wives.

Archetypes:
- Delilah chopping off Sampson's hair.
- Women using witchcraft or sorcery against men.
- Women cuckolding or scolding their husbands.
- Phyllis riding Aristotle.
- Salome requesting or receiving the head of John the Baptist.
- Judith beheading Holofernes while he sleeps.

It was used as a joke, really,
amongst men.

Of course Judith was a weak woman.
Yes, of course, I am also a weak woman.

I tried to write a ghost poem

It wasn't a failure, more
than any other
exercise of language

That's boring, though
        and I imagine a television set
            to keep us all entertained

I'd want to see a super bowl commercial
use puns to describe the systematic elimination
of strange women from public spaces

or use white men's bodies to raise awareness of violence
against black men's bodies

I'd like to see an explosion
mend the flesh and preserve the dark

A man named Increase, the father of HayStak
fathers of such misery
But he wasn't the father—I am

You can see my failure
in imagination and in begetting

And as you see
there are no real ghosts here

just dads

The Tower

The Tower was never
        something I feared
like a long enough day without   ample   water
or fear of snow

But at some point I
became worthy of retribution

It was a joy... *wasn't it?*

I threw off the clothes
of mourning, the drab prison
of clothes that
only existed in my mind

We will feast in the Hall of Kings tonight !
Laugh and sing until we choke on our tongues !

There is no governance without oppression
The governor concedes this fact but keeps his title
as hypocritical as any Founding Father

It falls, tho
it all falls it all all falls always

American Beauty

the computer doesn't know what I'm writing

my hand won't know when my head is dead

the internet does know that I'm a Gemini
they've already felt the cleaver come down
splitting everything in twain

I won't know until I'm properly Removed

a rich system of symbols leads easily from rain to my hatred of rain
my fear of language and the symbolism
inherent in both the male and female "form"

love being impossible when it's committed to this binary

the time of the Dead Land has come
as absurd and predictable as throwing yourself out the window

lousy with brunch in the Dead Land

a friend of the devil is a friend of mine, etc.

Look for America

Hunched over
eating a banana
over a trashy magazine

everything is trash
if you believe it

Nothing remained
of the mannequin besides her head
with a sequined hat
reading: SEXY

the indignities
of my own birth
 so loud
I hate to even think it

Mantra:
*Trash profligates widely
because I exist*

truth is not beauty and
beauty is not truth
and don't let dead white men lie to you like that ever again

What happens next
is as predictable
as a bad day

Baby Hole

Suffering is a long black Gown I put on when I want to feel
special and Listen to some Sabbath
Drink something straight out

Are any of us important ?
Deserving of love ?
A wave fighting its way onto the shore ?

//////

I don't want to write about bodies anymore
or the head being removed from the body
or the body destroyed
But language has its origins in its various ways to trap women
to punish them for justifiable acts
like breathing while dying

I'm afraid I must go on

//////

My mind is friendly and warm—
maybe even soft
It wants to lie somewhere comfortable
It thinks about recovery and tries
to recover

arms

        it's beauty that we
       are all after,
           hunting
                    it down like rabbit

words become exquisite
     in a bloom— but who

will listen ?

I want to be a tree

    a tree chopped down
        a world for pleasures—
            when really, a world so
                untenable that it's easy
                    to slip into its core

rather than a diamond

    the gulf is becoming the sea, isn't
        it ? We can't and
            should not drown   but Revolution *is* drowning
    does that mean we'll drown
    that I will, in fact, drown ? and

what comes after   that ?

I WANT MY BODY TO LAY SCREECHING after I'm dead. Men, men are writing about flowers right now. Fucking flowers. Flowers as a political act. I'm left. Or just my head is left. Telling you the same boring story. Over again.

VOID

My body is a diamond mine
which is to say
it causes great suffering

I'm afraid of my own handwriting
I think it might hurt people

I know my own Suffering is inevitable
I know that as I lay here
a scrap on the floor
that the promises of love
time and death are not meant
for me but I thought
the rest of you might've
been spared

I see now

I've written a death sentence

You'll come awake just in time
for the snack cart but
after that, it's over

it's over
it's overt

like opening the window in the Boeing 757
I'm pretty sure none of us can stay here
Mothers are looking now at children and dogs but I'm sorry
we will soon be looking
at only atmosphere

/\

I request that we pause a moment to consider *Judith Slaying Holofernes* composed by Artemisia Gentileschi dated between 1614-1620

It is notable for several reasons:

One, Judith's handmaiden, usually portrayed as a old woman in these sorts of paintings, is much younger and is actively engaged in the fight to kill Holofernes

Two, it depicts the violence and struggle and disgust that most definitely would accompany the act of decapitating a large man with a sword

(e.g. Holofernes' hand reaches for the handmaiden's throat as he dies)

Three, Gentileschi painted herself as Judith

Four, the painting was very clearly inspired by Caravaggio's *Judith Beheading Holofernes* but in Caravaggio's painting the violent blood bursting from Holofernes' major arteries seems to confuse his pretty Judith and her much older maid

Judith, here, proceeds single-mindedly, looking only slightly annoyed

Five, Holofernes was modeled after Agostino Tassi, Gentileschi's former mentor who was later tried in court for her rape (as well as murder of his wife and the incestual rape of his sister-in-law)

In which the protagonist eats naked unaware of certain tragedies:

The theory of the Wild Woman and the teachings of Madame Blavatsky were not far from my mind. The earth's cycles and the undiscoverable language. A woman who makes lots of decisions for lots of people heard a Fleetwood Mac song at a bar and needed to leave immediately, as if "bitten by a snake." Like Faust at his lover's grave. The protagonist barely remembered Faust but remembered The Devil and the Dead Lover quite well. How many times have I been killed by the soulless ? But the protagonist is Stevens' self-indulgent pagan. Dancing around the fires of I-don't-remember before Puritans put them out.

But seriously, we ask
what are you doing now ?
What have you done all day ?

Let us Pray

MIRACLE SONGS

...Once the general has been decapitated, there's no reason to complicate matters or split hairs, even less to leave them dirty, since that erotic frenzy is truly only a miserable attempt to remedy castration, as everyone knows.

-Julia Kristeva

a man is walking down the beach and there is no one for miles

when he comes across a woman with no arms or legs
she's just a torso and she's crying
why are you crying ? he asks
I'm 21 years old and I have no arms and no legs and I've never been kissed
hearing this, the man's heart just breaks and he leans down and kisses her
it's a tender moment
he continues walking when he hears her cry again
again he stops to ask her, *why are you crying ?*
I'm 21 years old and I have no arms and no legs and I've never been screwed
so he bends down, picks her up and throws her in the ocean and says,
you're screwed now

---

[1]Decapitation or beheading is the act of cutting off the head from the rest of the body.

...there was then discovered a connection between God's invisibility (or unavailability)
and the endowment of humans with a soul or divine component, longing for God

it had been there all along
since the first

---

²Suicide by decapitation is rare, but not unknown.

it is important to start with the face or defaced

reject the idea of head as penis
as the ultimate castration
If that is true, then a woman can't even be beheaded

It would be such a fucking waste

---

[3] It is where the term Capital Punishment came from, referring to the punishment for serious offences involving the forfeiture of the head.

I don't want to be *that* woman but I
am that woman as certain
as a hard truth that does not fade
in the light

I know I'll find them—
my aggressions—
again

---

[4]Remnants of 9,000-year-old beheadings were found in Brazil.

Cixous called it a punishment that *history keeps reserved for woman*

feminine disorder, its laughter, its inability to take the drumbeat seriously.

is this, then, a chance for a new female species
many-headed
trans-phallic?

for Kristeva has also said it was the distinct fate for women in a patriarchal society

A COMPLETE SILENCE

there has been a systematic attempt to keep women's heads separate from their body.

    (emphasis mine)

---

[5]The executioner would often hold the head up to the crowd. Partially as proof, but partially to rile the crowd up. Public Executions were often social events. People brought picnic baskets.

Carlton's last thoughts, unspoken,
are prophetic

The villain is also the victim but caught
in the horrible cycle of
multi-generational retribution

like tossing the heart into the fire and severing the head

---

[5] Your leader is also your Head of State, since the State is a body. Our leader is our head. Remove the Head and we die. From the Latin for dead *caput*- hence *capitis*.

bodies are vulnerable
miraculous
wounds heal so quickly

one does not learn devotion like this

go down into the valley
love someone you cannot see

additionally, love no one you *can* see

whoever thought we were fine
is wrong

---

[6]The King of Dahomey cuts off the heads of 127 people to complete the ornamentation on his wall in 1793.

I'm not superstitious
but I did see what happened

the man, decapitated, walked past
ten maybe twelve men before
he was tripped by the executioner
and fell to his true death

a testament to the loyalty of a criminal
gone for good
smothered by the shore

a man truly repairing himself

---

[8]Abraham would have decapitated his own son Isaac to please the Lord.

we know, though, that death isn't
peaceful it isn't even

oblivion, what
do you want out of this anyway ?
a souvenir ? a trophy ?
or a warning ?

a figure can so easily tip over the balustrade
a figure cut against the dusk
we only have stupid
questions

I am a singing/shitting momento mori
everything decomposes in me
reminding you
that you, no matter how powerful
or rich, or brave—

you will die, most certainly
the seat of your soul will be vacated
your body, thus, garbage

---

[9]For Plato the head was representative of the Rational part of the soul. The universe is a product of rational agency. The immortal and rational soul, in fact, is physically located in the head. The head, therefore, being the closest to the Divine.

that is the thing
about miracles—
they do not care
about you
they do not care

only the hard
aspect of the
miracle against
the corrupt flesh

you will perform
miracles but you
will then die
that is all
I can guarantee

---

[10]Humans invented decapitation as a form of death. Accidental decapitations, say, when a cat is toying with a mouse, will happen, but the cat does not do it purposefully. Some would posit that it proves our love of symbolism. In fact, group violence may have been the first symbolic act of humanity.

Decollation

For traitors on the block should die;
I am no traitor, no, not I!
My faithfulness stands fast and so,
Towards the block I shall not go!
Nor make one step, as you shall see;
Christ in Thy Mercy, save Thou me!

-Anne Boleyn

Prisoner, in this solemn hour, when all eyes are upon thee, and thy judges are jubilant, and thou art preparing for those involuntary bodily movements that directly follow severance of the head, I address to thee a parting word.

-Vladimir Nabokov

A page of mourning

Cut off her head before she casts a spell on   You are Queen of Nothing
I told you she was a   witch Cut   off her head It is now that she will
live   her days   There are few   pleasures   like seeing
a beautiful   woman naked   Cut off her head
                  (naked before us)

cut

off

her

head

Agnes of Rome

Agnus, Latin for lamb
Anus, pink
stars, bright

Agnes, the Object of desire
(and the reason we are here today)
holding in herself *no desire*
beyond a passionate yearning of devotion
to the Christ Child

And so it is
the Unwanting Wanted
dragged naked by the hair through Roman brothels

the fires all went out
so they lopped off her head

It's the old story
so old
we've forgotten it entirely

Medusa

Let me hold
you

hand, hair, cock, coat
any of it

let me hold
you

until you turn
to stone

Just surrender
yourself

to the emotional
abuse
of loving
a woman who
was never that
pretty

I am Jeanne

I am Jeanne d'Arc
The Eternal Spirit here
taking longer to do the dishes
since all that is left
are the complicated dishes

Men hate it when women talk to god
When god chooses women to talk to
This is why I'm eternally reborn
rather than immortal

there will be no help (for the kingdom) if not from me
Children say that people are halved sometimes for speaking the truth

My boyfriend and I got
each other the same thing for Christmas:
    SALVATION

It was embarrassing but totally worth it

Fertility

Imagine the red Sun Orb
Imagine it radiating from inside
Radiating from what once
connected you to woman—
now radiating with the sun's rays

Two sisters cut off their own sister
Cut off their own heads presenting
them to their teacher
then danced standing
on the bodies of a copulating couple

My lolling tongue makes
them uncomfortable
and my undone hair
or no, matronly hair and headlessness

Why do up your hair
if you are only going to cut off your own head ?

The Cult of the Head

Fertile chaos, for sure, but,
this all just doesn't begin

It doesn't spring out of the spray

It has always existed

Before the earth, there was the bloody head
the sun in the sky—
someone's murdered brother

We needed his death

like we need the deaths of the Saints
to prove that God loves us

We are all potentially
the Lamb and the Slaughter
in the sun/are the sun

Everyone was afraid that they'd die

Some did, but not as much as
the fear of pain and death
and pain of death

It's cute to be an American poet obsessed with death
knowing, like Wilfred Owen, that death
does not mean quiet or peace

<u>Nevertheless.</u>

some time ago I was drenched
with my own sweat
when my father had me chopped to pieces
as punishment for my beliefs
(most of which I've forgotten)
He had both arms detached from my body
My tongue said all sorts
of nasty things—
so much so that he dumped
all of me in the ocean but not
before he had that tongue ripped out
The ocean was thirty miles away
meaning I didn't arrive at the shore
for two months
He squashed my little
eyes thinking that would
truly blind me
but I crawled back— not
out of love, but for the power of living

It went on this way for hundreds
of years until my father died, then
my eldest brother was murdered
by an especially enterprising cousin
only to be murdered by my poor

sister who ended up as an excellent ruler
She ruled alone until she was forced to marry
an old German idiot
with a boatload of gold
that would have restored our suffering empire to
whatever incestuous
glory, but the boat sank
and the dukes murdered the pair
The dukes in turn were murdered
by some grandnephew of mine
and he ruled in relative
peace until the whole family line
was wiped out by a headless orange giant
with a magic axe

It was boring
surviving as such—
an eternal scrap

I had a thought, and here I am

Shitting as a political act
nudity as vanity
decaying rapidly and poorly

A gaudy and decrepit end
to life that leads
further on
somewhere

When the king is murdered and reborn
all we get is another year
an infinite lineup of days
waiting patiently
to corrupt the incorruptible landscape

How many wars are happening now, you lovers of peace ?

I didn't mean to love or consume
anything, but there are
crumbs on my shirt

These emblems mean
new beginnings brought
about by correct action

I dreamt of wearing headphones
and nothing was coming out of them
but air and I woke up
on an airplane watching people
eat breakfast
From up here pine trees look like dirt

Some Experiments with Severed Heads

I know what you're thinking
and I agree

I'm also afraid
and slightly cold

After so many hours here
here with us together
I wonder where my respect for the dead has gone

Flesh was never sacred
It seems silly to have to say it at all

That was not the point of any gospel
In fact, it is so easy to destroy a whole town of people

Dickens (at the Paris morgue): *I was looking at something that could not return a look*

A night to dismember

I'm in love with the moments
before the axe falls
where we wonder about
how much pain we will feel
before passing out or dying

he opens his yellow eyes
he tells me his body is rotting
but I am his body
I tell him so and start
my rapid decline

It is worth acknowledging

I still have my head

but not the time I wasted
trying to turn objects into gold

I got lost
in the Black Forest

I am no longer
able to look on with love

No longer able to feel
that delightful sensitivity
to the ever-present dangers

Time passes
even more quickly when it's cold

It's a freezing thought, I know
first snow, then snow

then letting go

Believe what I say

ALIVE or DEAD
that girl is carried along endlessly
sleeping late, PLEASING
herself endlessly and others

But now, her head rolls
and where it stops, a spring appears
scarlet swings and dances on the blade

SO BE IT
Thou steal
thou butcher

Her head, sheared
from her shoulders, FELL
down the beetling banks, like water
in waterfalls

It stopped and flashed and fell and ran like water away.

AND I DO NOT REPENT;
I do NOT and I WILL NOT REPENT, NOT REPENT.
The blame bear aroused me.
What I have done violent
I have like a lion done

*(Cardaroc fell down dead on the spot
And the ground opened up to swallow him)*

for not in róck
but in pale water, frail water, wild rash and reeling water,
Thy venerable record, Virgin, is recorded

Music Minus One High Voice:

I sat on, listening, since I am a miracle
I created a miracle
I was witness to a miracle
I was beheaded but lived
spreading the word of miracle
across the world
until a freak traffic accident
sent me into the Iguazu Falls
scarf flapping in the wind

(No one wants you to die, so you won't)

The _____ of Lucretia

JUNIUS: Love, like wine,
spills easily as blood.

TARQUINIUS:
And men are the broken bottles

LUCRETIA, BIANCA, LUCIA: Death is woman's final lover,
in whose arms we lie forever
with our hearts all broken.

BIANCA: So it is.
I can almost hear my thinking.

LUCRETIA: And what are you thinking?

BIANCA: That it must be men, who make the noise.

FEMALE CHORUS: Through all man's art, there runs this paradox:
passion for creation and lust to kill.
Behind the swan's neck they'd paint a fox,
and on their tombs a wooden phallus stood.

MALE CHORUS: All tyrants fall,
though tyranny persists.
Though crowds disperse,
the mob is never less.

TARQUINIUS: Loveliness like this is never chaste!
If not enjoyed, it is such a waste!

LUCRETIA: No!
What you have taken, was never given!

TARQUINIUS: Loveliness like this cannot be chaste
unless all men are blind!

Poised like a dart!

LUCRETIA: At the heart of woman.

MALE CHORUS: Man climbs towards his God.

FEMALE CHORUS: Then falls to his lonely hell.

LUCRETIA: Take them away, I tell you!
Oh, monstrous flower!
Oh, hideous hour!

COLLATINUS: To love, as we loved,
was to live on the edge of tragedy:
To love, as we loved,
was to live on the edge of tragedy.

[LUCRETIA *dies*]

EVERYTHING I DO IS A STATEMENT ABOUT HOW I'M GOING TO LIVE FOREVER

We are you
We are young and borish
We are young and bored and life is so long

If you are going to love your brother
at least do so passionately

If you are already giving
If you are already a saint

Eventually we just swallow our tongue

The question you need to ask yourself is

It takes dynamite to get me up

She emerged from the sea
with her head in hands

& according to this
she was a pious girl who was merely the victim
of a jealous stepmother

Upon the death of her father
she began to suffer a pain in her chest
Its source was ascribed
to her sorrow and austerities

whereupon immediately they
struck off her head

She held two rabid dogs at bay
with the power of her saintly voice

She was beheaded on the spot

Her mother, disgusted
by the fact that she had given birth to 9 daughters
all at once as if she were
a common peasant (or an animal)
ordered a maid to take them to a river
to drown them

A rock opened up and swallowed
her and on the spot
there sprang up a hot spring

Her husband ran off to hunt a beautiful white stag

She stood up after her execution
and picked up her dead head
bringing it to the convent before collapsing

A fig tree grew from her staff

She picked up her head and,
led by her maid, returned to England

The head was thrown into a furnace
was lapidated
and was thrown to a lion or a panther at
an amphitheater

A spring of water appeared at the spot

She walked forty paces uphill, and prayed
before lying down in death

Townspeople spilled snails
on the road and she stepped on them
without breaking one

She invoked the heavens
and a lightning bolt hit the ground
near her captors

Nevertheless, her limbs were
amputated and she was beheaded

Revenge Head

When Cyrus was killed, Tomyris had his corpse beheaded and then crucified. Shoving his head into a wineskin filled with human blood, she is reportedly quoted as saying, *I warned you that I would quench your thirst for blood, and so I shall*

Lots of people have been thirsty
for such a long time
and we do things
like build structures
entertain people for dinner
create an atmosphere

The Head at the End of the Mind

I have a deep need
to insert myself
to identify the situation and produce
my tongue—
flat, wet, covered in bumps
I have one and here it is

I went to the store and couldn't
find caraway seeds
but I did find the entire head of a cow
decaying exactly as you would think
behind the butcher's glass case

I think you will find
that it spoke to me that it said
to me my true thoughts and feelings
and not just *moo* which
it also just did

You're afraid that you're a failure
said the cow head and *we*
know this to be true
people only love you out of habit
but there is something extraordinary
about you and not just life or living
or vitality but you are lamb's
blood on the doorway
you guarantee safe
passage to all those who know you
you are water from a cactus
you are the camel's hump
you are the steak that distracts the dog's of hell
you must stay alive

The Executioner's Song

Executions are often ordered,
seldom stayed
No salt
remembrance of a steady, falling rate
a falling grate

I made some very serious promises
to engineer my own reality
ignoring the Brothers who look so much like me, it's scary

It is sharp, right ?
Blades have been sharpened ?
Hair cut too close
knicked the skin
The fear of immortality
but rather too tall to live forever

Clearing up our decimated youths
Friends of Justice rejoice !
All that exists is naturally drunk !

Reprise:
- Things as themselves
- Things in and of themselves
- The body, quartered
- The head, missing
- The head, removed from the rest of the body
- The day, a long fuck
- And the night of that day
- Our youth was also doomed

Salome Requesting the Head of John the Baptist on a Plate

The Voice Calling in the Wilderness
Prepare Ye the Way of the Lord
etc.

It's remarkable

The Voice is the Word
We don't see him
so his body never existed

      So what exactly is her crime ?

What I really mean to get at with all of this:

is that it is so easy
for the life force
      to leave a body

You just ask for it
& it happens

An Invitation to a Beheading

but no one has to die

there's no reason
to lie there
awaiting the blade
there is no reason for it

don't
die

every morning I whisper that into your ear
as you go to war
war after pointless war

don't
die

please

don't

die

NOTES

THE SAINTS ARE DEAD is a series of poems composed using the words written by and about historical beheading victims. Each poem title is in reference to the day in which they were murdered, according to the French Revolutionary Calendar, a system that gives each individual day of the year its own unique name, in reference to common objects. This was thought to be a true democratization of the calendar, stripping them of their Roman or Norse mythological origins. The date and location, which serve as the post-script for each poem, are where and when each decapitation occurred. I have been asked why I don't reveal the victims' names in the poems themselves. More-so then any other act of violence, decapitation is an act of silencing. I want to focus on the words rather then the biography. The subject of each poem is listed below:

WHEAT: Charlotte Corday, Marat's assassin.
RAKE: Anna Zippel, a Swedish woman accused of witchcraft.
OX: Marie Antoinette, Queen of France.
LEADWORTS: Madame Roland, aristocrat and political influencer.
GARLIC: Qui Jin, Chinese writer and revolutionary.
PRIVET: Sophie Scholl, German Resistance member.
HATCHERY: Maria Restituta Kafka, Austrian nurse and nun.
HELLBORE: Kenji Goto, Japanese journalist, captured by ISIS.

THE DEVIL'S OWN takes texts from the IMDB descriptions of the Brad Pitt film, *The Devil's Own*.

THE LABOR OF BEING contains several lines from John Berger's *And Our Faces, My Heart, Brief as Photos* describing Van Gogh.

IN WHICH THE PROTAGONIST EATS NAKED UNAWARE OF CERTAIN TRAGEDIES: "Wild Women," refers to *Women Who Run with Wolves*, which I recommend to any woman-identifying person reading this. Also Helen Cixous' *Reveries of a Wild Woman*. Madame

Blavatsky was influential clairvoyant and mystical teacher and writer.

A MAN IS WALKING DOWN THE BEACH AND THERE IS NO ONE FOR MILES is taken directly from Season 1, Episode 9 of *Ally McBeal*. In the episode, Ally and her roommate Rene engage in a wager over who can tell the best dirty joke at the bar. This is a transcription of the joke that Rene tells to uproarious laughter.

BELIEVE WHAT I SAY reassembled and edited text taken from the "St. Winnifred's Well" by Gerard Manley Hopkins.

MUSIC MINUS ONE HIGH VOICE includes biographical details from the life of Madelena Delani, the Romanian-American opera singer who died tragically in a car crash in Igazu Falls. There is an excellent permanent exhibition at the Museum of Jurassic Technology in Los Angeles that explores her life and music in relation to intersecting memories.
http://www.mjt.org/exhibits/delson/delani.html

THE ____ OF LUCRETIA is taken from the libretto of Benjamin Britten's *The Rape of Lucretia*.

IT TAKES DYNAMITE TO GET ME UP is taken from a series of Wikipedia pages about female saints called "Head Carriers," named such since they miraculously picked up and carried their heads after decapitation.

THE EXECUTIONER'S SONG contains a line from Helen Cixous' *Stigmata*.

Christine Kanownik is the author of *KING OF PAIN* (Monk Books, 2016) and the chapbook *We Are Now Beginning to Act Wildly* (Diez, 2012). Her poems, art, or writing have appeared in *The Huffington Post, Fence, Motherboard, EOAGH, jubilat*, among others. She currently lives and works in Chicago.

ACKNOWLEDGEMENTS

Love to Brett, always.

Thank you to Megan Burns and the rest of the team at Trembling Pillow Press for working so diligently on making this book a reality.

And thanks to the artists Rachel Stern and James Lyman for so generously allowing me to use their artwork on the cover.

Thank you to the editors of *Diagram, Gramma, Big Lucks, Cosmonauts Avenue*, and *Bone Bouquet* for publishing some of these poems in their journals or magazines.

And thanks to Allison Power, Amy Lawless, Paul Legault, Sharmila Cohen, Jessica Madison, Lauren Hunter, Joe Giovannetti, Jennifer Nelson, Diana Arterian, and Jeff T. Johnson, for reading versions of this manuscript, supporting my work, and keeping me from giving up, which I am always threatening to do.

Trembling Pillow Press

I of the Storm by Bill Lavender
Olympia Street by Michael Ford
Ethereal Avalanche by Gina Ferrara
Transfixion by Bill Lavender
Downtown by Lee Meitzen Grue
SONG OF PRAISE   Homage To John Coltrane by John Sinclair
DESERT JOURNAL by ruth weiss
Aesthesia Balderdash by Kim Vodicka
SUPER NATURAL by Tracey McTague
I LOVE THIS AMERICAN WAY OF LIFE by Brett Evans
loaded arc by Laura Goldstein
Want for Lion by Paige Taggart
Trick Rider by Jen Tynes
May Apple Deep by Michael Sikkema
Gossamer Lid by Andrew Brezna
simple constructs for the lizzies by Lisa Cattrone
FILL: A Collection by Kate Schapira and Erika Howsare
Red of Split Water a burial rite by Lisa Donovan
CUNTRY by Kristin Sanders
Kids of the Black Hole by Marty Cain
Feelings by Lauren Ireland
If You Love Error So Love Zero by Stephanie Anderson
The Boneyard, The Birth Manual, A Burial: Investigations into the Heartland by Julia Madsen
You've Got A Pretty Hellmouth by Michael Sikkema
HEAD by Christine Kanownik

Forthcoming Titles:

Unoriginal Danger by Dominique Salas
Book of Levitatons by Anne Champion and Jenny Sadre-Orafai
marginal utility by Tracey McTague

Trembling Pillow Press

Bob Kaufman Book Prize

2012: *Of Love & Capital* by Christopher Rizzo (Bernadette Mayer, judge)

2013: *Psalms for Dogs and Sorcerers* by Jen Coleman (Dara Wier, judge)

2014: *Natural Subjets* by Divya Victor (Anselm Berrigan, judge)

2015: *there are boxes and there is wanting* by Tessa Micaela Landreau-Grasmuck (Laura Mullen, judge)

2016 *orogeny* by Irène Mathieu (Megan Kaminski, judge)

Please visit tremblingpillowpress.com for details on our new book prize in honor of poet Marthe Reed.

NEW ORLEANS

www.ingramcontent.com/pod-product-compliance
Lightning Source LLC
Chambersburg PA
CBHW022117090426
42743CB00008B/896